UPDOG

IN THE SPOTLIGHT

TYLER "NINJA" BLEVINS

PRO GAMING STAR

Heather E. Schwartz

Lerner Publications ◆ Minneapolis

This book is dedicated to all the gamers out there.

Lerner Publications Company
An imprint of Lerner Publishing Group, Inc.
241 First Avenue North
Minneapolis, MN 55401 USA

For reading levels and more information, look up this title at www.lernerbooks.com.

Main body text set in ITC Franklin Gothic Std.
Typeface provided by Adobe Systems.

Designer: Viet Chu

Library of Congress Cataloging-in-Publication Data

Names: Schwartz, Heather E., author.
Title: Tyler "Ninja" Blevins: pro gaming star / Heather E. Schwartz.
Description: Minneapolis : Lerner Publications , [2023] | Series: In the Spotlight (UpDog Books) | Includes bibliographical references and index. | Audience: Ages 8–11 years | Audience: Grades 4–6 | Summary: "Tyler "Ninja" Blevins rose to fame as a professional gamer. Taking esports competitions by storm and racking up fans by streaming on Twitch, Ninja dominates the gaming world and shows no signs of slowing down!"— Provided by publisher.
Identifiers: LCCN 2021039659 (print) | LCCN 2021039660 (ebook) | ISBN 9781728458335 (Library Binding) | ISBN 9781728461786 (eBook)
Subjects: LCSH: Blevins, Tyler, 1991—-Juvenile literature. | Video gamers—Biography—Juvenile literature.
Classification: LCC GV1469.3.B58 S3 2022 (print) | LCC GV1469.3.B58 (ebook) | DDC 794.8092 [B]—dc23

LC record available at https://lccn.loc.gov/2021039659
LC ebook record available at https://lccn.loc.gov/2021039660

Manufactured in the United States of America
1-50862-50199-11/17/2021

TABLE OF CONTENTS

Growing Up Gaming

Tyler Blevins screamed with joy. *Fortnite* got a Ninja skin! It made a character in the game look just like him.

skin: a graphic that changes a character's appearance

Tyler grew up playing video games with his brothers.

Tyler's mom said the boys couldn't game all day. They had to get good grades and hold jobs.

When Tyler played video games, he wanted to win. He was the best gamer in his family.

UP NEXT!

Going pro.

Pro Player

Great gamers can win prize money at esports events. Tyler knew he had what it takes. He decided to get in the game.

After high school, he went pro. He focused on *Halo*. He played for several different teams.

Tyler used the name Ninja when he played.

At events, Tyler helped his teams win.
Before long, he was an esports champion.

STAR STATS

Full name: Richard Tyler "Ninja" Blevins

Date of birth: June 5, 1991

Hometown: Chicago, Illinois

HONORS:

Became the first Twitch streamer to reach ten million followers

Won the 2018 *Fortnite* Celebrity Pro-Am tournament

Was the first esports player to appear on the cover of *ESPN* magazine in 2018

Tyler also started streaming his gameplay. Fans enjoyed watching him play.

streaming: sending content to devices for people to watch

Tyler put all of his time into streaming. He started earning more than $100 a day.

UP NEXT!

Becoming the best.

Top of His Game

In 2017, a new game came out.
Tyler started playing *Fortnite*.

In 2018, he played with the rapper Drake. A huge crowd tuned in.

Tyler streamed about four thousand hours of gameplay in 2018.

Playing games made Tyler rich.
He gives money away to help others.

Tyler has talent. He hopes to do more with it. He says movies might be in his future!

Just like Ninja

Tyler "Ninja" Blevins practiced a lot to reach the top. What's one of your most important goals? What steps could you take to reach it?

GLOSSARY

esports: professional competitive gaming

skin: a graphic that changes a character's appearance

streaming: sending content to devices for people to watch

CHECK IT OUT!

Furgang, Adam. *Tyler "Ninja" Blevins: Twitch's Top Streamer with 11 Million+ Followers*. New York: Rosen Central, 2020.

Gardiner, Nora. *Tyler "Ninja" Blevins*. New York: Enslow, 2022.

Owings, Lisa. *Pro Gaming*. Minneapolis: Lerner Publications, 2021.

Polinsky, Paige V. *Fortnite*. Minneapolis: Checkerboard Library, 2020.

Rusick, Jessica. *Ninja*. Minneapolis: Checkerboard Library, 2020.

INDEX

PHOTO ACKNOWLEDGMENTS

Image credits: Cassiano Correia/Shutterstock.com, p. 4; Robert Reiners/Stringer/Getty Images, pp. 5, 11, 15; 4 PM production/Shutterstock.com, p. 6; Bryan Bedder/Stringer/Getty Images, p. 7; Johannes Eisele/AFP/Getty Images, p. 8; Miguel Lagoa/Shutterstock.com, pp. 9, 16; AP Photo/Ryan Scott Hadji/Red Bull via AP Images, p. 10; Gary I Rothstein/UPI/Shutterstock.com, p. 12; MPH Photos/Shutterstock.com, p. 14; Prince Williams/Wireimage/Getty Images, p. 17; Ethan Miller/Staff/Getty Images, p. 18; Brace Hemmelgarn/Minnesota Twins/Getty Images, p. 19; Theo Wargo/Staff/Getty Images, p. 20. Design Elements: Medesulda/Getty Images; oxygen/Getty Images.

Cover: Gary I Rothstein/UPI/Shutterstock.com.